Healthy Eating
for Kids

Healthy Eating
for Kids

A fun and informative guide to family wellbeing

igloo

Published in 2009
by Igloo Books Ltd
Cottage Farm
Sywell
NN6 0BJ
www.igloo-books.com

10 9 8 7 6 5 4 3 2

ISBN: 978-1-84561-890-2

Printed and manufactured in China

Designed by
THE BRIDGEWATER BOOK COMPANY

Jupiter Images/E. Jane Armstrong 35 (far left) and 44; Jupiter Images/Mary Ellen Bartley 17 (far right), 32, 35 (2nd from left) and 47; Jupiter Images/Leigh Beisch 35 (2nd from right) and 50; Jupiter Images/Burke/Triolo Productions 10, 15 (bottom), 35 (middle), 48, 76 (far left) and 78; Jupiter Images/Jon Burwell 15 (top), 34 (far left) and 36; Jupiter Images/Renee Comet 77 (2nd from left) and 89; Jupiter Images/Steve Cohen 13 (far right); Jupiter Images/Eisenhut & Mayer 11 (top right); Jupiter Images/Rob Fiocca 35 (far right), 53, 55 (far left) and 67; Istock/Jose Manuel Gelpi Diaz 9 (bottom);stock/Jose Manuel Gelpi Diaz 9 (bottom);Jupiter Images/Brian Hagiwara 34 (2nd from right) and 41; Istock 9 (top); Jupiter Images/ Spencer Jones 76 (2nd from left) and 81; Jupiter Images/ Richard Jung 76 (2nd from right) and 83; Jupiter Images 77 (far left) and 86; Jupiter Images/John E. Kelly 77 (middle) and 91; Jupiter Images/Kathryn Kleinman 11 (left); Jupiter Images/Rick Lew 14; Istock/Olga Lyubkina 7; Jupiter Images/Randy Mayor 54 (2nd from left) and 59; Jupiter Images/Gary Moss 34 (far left) and 43; Jupiter Images/Steven Mark Needham 17 (far left), 26, 55 (2nd from right) and 72; Jupiter Images/Scott Payne 17 (2nd from left) and 29; Istock/ Denis Pepin 6 (top); Jupiter Images/David Prince 13 (bottom), 77 (2nd from right) and 92; Jupiter Images/Judd Pilossof 16 (2nd from left) and 22; Jupiter Images/Michael Piazza 55 (2nd from left) and 69; Jupiter Images/Heath Robbins 16 (far left) and 19; Jupiter Images/ Lew Robertson 11 (bottom right) and 13 (2nd from left); Jupiter Images/Evan Sklar 55 (far right) and 75; Jupiter Images/Shimon & Tammar 54 (middle) and 60; Jupiter Images/Ann Stratton 54 (2nd from right), 55 (middle), 63 and 70; Jupiter Images/ Mark Thomas 13 (2 and 3 from right); Jupiter Images/James Tse Photography Inc. 54 (far right) and 64; Istock/Graça Victoria 34 (far left background) and 36 (background); Jupiter Images/Elizabeth Watt 16 (far right), 17 (2nd from right), 20 and 31; Jupiter Images/Simon Watson 16 (2nd from right) and 25; Jupiter Images/Wendell Webber 77 (far right) and 94; Jupiter Images/Kurt Wilson 34 (2nd from left), 38, 54 (far left), 57, 76 (far right) and 85; Jupiter Images/Stephen Wisbauer 13(far left);Istock/Nicole S. Young 6 (bottom).

contents

Healthy eating

What exactly do we mean by healthy eating? Put simply, most experts, including the World Health Organization, agree that we all need to eat a minimum of five portions of fruit and vegetables each day to help maintain a good standard of health. This applies just as much to children as it does to adults.

The emphasis in this book is on ensuring your child gets his or her recommended daily intake of fruit and vegetables. There are lots of reasons why fruit and vegetables are so good for you, but the most important one is that they are full of nutrients that are vital to a healthy body.

Many fruit and vegetables are rich sources of vitamins A and C, potassium, magnesium, and folic acid. In addition, these foods are rich in antioxidants—substances that counter the negative effects of oxygen in the body. They help the body to protect itself against premature aging. They are also good for the heart and circulation,

and help to protect cells from damage from potentially harmful pollutants, such as food additives and pesticides.

Fruit and vegetables are low in fat and are good sources of fiber, which helps maintain a healthy digestive system and prevent bowel problems such as constipation and diarrhea.

Various surveys have shown that adults who ate fruit and vegetables regularly during their childhood had a lower incidence of cancer than adults who didn't eat them. If you consume a wide range of different types of fruit and vegetables, you will ensure that you and your children get the complete range of minerals and vitamins that you need.

Five a day and your baby

Try to get your child into the five-a-day habit as early as you can. Babies are at an ideal age for this: they are often willing to try new foods, whereas children of two years plus are often less adventurous. Try puréeing fruit, or steaming and puréeing vegetables. Apples, pears, bananas, carrots, broccoli, potatoes, and zucchini (courgettes) are all suitable.

As your child gets older, introduce other fruit and vegetables, such as avocado, melon, cauliflower, tomatoes, and grapes (remove the seeds). If giving citrus fruit, peel, and remove the pith and seeds.

Five a day and your child

You can also introduce an older child to the five-a-day habit—it just needs patience, and remember to make it fun. In this book you'll find plenty of quick, nutritious, and simple recipes packed with essential nutrients to boost your child's well-being.

A good way to get your child to eat more fruit and vegetables is to offer them as snacks throughout the day. Many children like to "graze," eating a little food here and there to boost their energy levels. These snacks could be as simple as a midmorning apple or banana or handful of berries, a salad sandwich, or a small package of dried apricots.

HOW MUCH IS A PORTION?

Here is a guide to help you calculate how much your child will need. The quantities listed are based on the requirements of a child aged ten or over. On the wallchart that accompanies this book, you will find a wider range of fruit and vegetables listed. Younger children and babies will need smaller portions. Use your child's appetite as a guide, but you will need to increase the portions as he or she grows. A useful way to judge this is to give your child the amount that he or she can hold in one hand.

Fruit
Apple: fresh, 1 medium
Apricots: dried, 3 whole
Banana: 1 medium
Grapes: 1 handful
Peach: fresh, 1 medium
Pear: fresh, 1 medium
Plums: 2 medium
Strawberries: 7 medium

Vegetables
Avocado: half
Broccoli: 2 largish florets
Carrot: 1 large
Cherry tomatoes: 7
Zucchini (courgette): half a large one
Green (French) beans: 4 heaping tbsp
Parsnip: 1 large
Peas (fresh, frozen, or canned): 3 heaping tbsp

Recipes that contain 2 or more portions of your five a day are marked with this symbol for an at-a-glance reference.

What is a healthy diet?

Fruit and vegetables are a vital part of a healthy diet, but your child also needs other foods in order to ensure a balanced diet that contains all the necessary nutrients. These pages explain what your child requires.

There are five important food groups, and you should choose enough foods from each group to ensure that your child's diet has everything it needs to maintain a good standard of health. The groups are: protein, carbohydrates, fats, vitamins, and minerals. Fiber and water are also essential in your daily diet. No nutrient works alone—each depends on the presence of others to be most effective.

Protein, carbohydrates, and fats are known as macronutrients, while vitamins and minerals are known as micronutrients, needed only in tiny amounts, but essential for normal growth and health. When broken down, carbohydrates and fats supply energy, while protein, in addition to energy, provides structural components required for cell growth and repair.

Protein

Protein is essential for health and supplies the building blocks for the body. It helps to build muscle and tissue, and therefore plays a very important role in your child's growth and development.

There are two types of protein: animal protein or high biological value (HBV) protein, and vegetable or low biological value (LBV) protein. HBV protein is found in meat, poultry, fish, eggs, milk, yogurt, and cheese, whereas LBV protein can be found in beans, grains, nuts, and seeds. The building blocks for protein are amino acids. HBV proteins contain all of what are known as the essential amino acids (ones which are not made in your body and have to come from food), whereas LBV may have some missing. However, combining vegetable protein from two different sources can still yield a total mix of all the essential amino acids. A good example of this is a peanut butter sandwich.

Carbohydrates

Over half of the daily intake of food should come from carbohydrates. These are the chief source of energy for all body functions. There are two types of carbohydrate: simple, and complex. Complex carbohydrates take longer for the body to break down and the slower-burning energy they provide is released more gradually, which is ideal for better-quality, longer-lasting energy.

Simple carbohydrates are sugars, most commonly consumed as sweet foods, such as cakes, desserts, candies (sweets), and sodas (fizzy drinks). They are released into the body quite quickly, giving fast-burning energy, but they have no nutritional value and are also

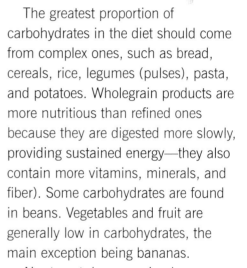

damaging to teeth. Other simple sugars are found (as lactose) in milk and milk products, and fructose, found in fruit. These are digested a little differently in the body and do not have the same effect on the teeth as ordinary sugar or sucrose.

The greatest proportion of carbohydrates in the diet should come from complex ones, such as bread, cereals, rice, legumes (pulses), pasta, and potatoes. Wholegrain products are more nutritious than refined ones because they are digested more slowly, providing sustained energy—they also contain more vitamins, minerals, and fiber). Some carbohydrates are found in beans. Vegetables and fruit are generally low in carbohydrates, the main exception being bananas.

Aim to cut down on simple carbohydrates and include more complex carbohydrates in your child's diet for optimum energy and performance. This is one of the main reasons why experts recommend eating more bread, cereals, rice, and pasta, and to restrict your intake of sugary foods, drinks, and desserts.

Fats

There has been an enormous amount of publicity these days about fat. We are constantly told that, if we eat it in excessive amounts, it won't just make us put on too much weight, it can also cause a variety of medical conditions and illnesses, such as high blood pressure and heart disease. As a result, experts everywhere are encouraging us to restrict our fat intake and switch to foods that are lower in fat.

However, things are not as simple as that because not all fats are bad. Your child needs a certain amount of fat because, along with carbohydrates and protein, fat is a useful energy source for the body. It also helps to improve the taste of the foods your child eats. Fats are also critical for normal brain development and nerve function. So what you really need to do is cut down on the potentially harmful fats, and replace them with healthier fats in your child's diet.

WHAT ARE HARMFUL FATS?

The potentially harmful fats are saturated fats and trans fatty acids (trans fats). It is often easy to recognize saturated fats because they tend to stay solid at room temperature. Fats that fall into this category include butter and lard, and are found in many fast foods. Saturated fats are also found in foods such as meat, cheese, whole milk, cream, and coconut oil.

Trans fats have also been linked with obesity, and are said to lower the levels of good cholesterol in the body and increase levels of bad cholesterol (this is another fatlike substance that can clog the arteries and restrict blood flow). Trans fats can be found in processed foods, such as cakes, cookies, and deep-fried foods.

The key here is moderation: do not try to make your child cut out these fats altogether, simply restrict them to smaller amounts.

FOCUS ON HEALTHIER FATS

It is also important to remember that some fats are not only harmless, they are actually good for your child. There are two main kinds of healthier fat: monounsaturated fats and polyunsaturated fats. These fats tend to be liquid at room temperature.

Monounsaturated fats can help protect against heart disease and are known to help lower cholesterol levels in the body. Rich sources of this fat include olive oil, peanut (groundnut) oil, avocados, sesame seeds, pumpkin seeds, almonds, Brazil nuts, hazelnuts, and peanuts.

Polyunsaturated fats are another kind of healthier fat and can be found in sunflower oil, corn oil, and soybean oil.

Essential fatty acids, present in some polyunsaturated fats, are needed in the diet and a deficiency in these can cause health problems. They are believed to

fight inflammation, lower blood pressure and bad cholesterol, and protect the nervous system and the brain. Rich sources of these fatty acids are sunflower seeds and sunflower oil. Omega-3 fatty acids are found in fish oils and to some extent in linseed (flax seed) and its oil. Omega-3 fatty acids are particularly important for the healthy development of your child's brain and nervous system.

FATS AND YOUR CHILD

When you are planning your child's diet, it is important to remember that children under five years need a lot more fat to boost their rapid growth, so a diet that is low in fat is unsuitable for them.

However, a lower-fat diet is perfectly acceptable for an older child, and there are many ways you can replace bad fats with good fats in your child's diet. Try any or all of the following:

● Replace bags of high-fat potato chips (crisps) with bags of healthier unsalted nuts, or dried fruits such as apricots and raisins.

● Replace butter with olive oil spreads.

● Switch to lower-fat alternatives of milk, yogurt, and cheese.

● Trim excess fat from meat, and remove the skin from poultry.

● Encourage your child to eat fresh fruit between meals instead of chocolates and candies (sweets).

● Give your child mackerel and salmon: they are rich in essential fatty acids and will help protect your child's health.

Vitamins

Your child also needs a good supply of vitamins and if he or she eats a wide variety of foods from all five groups, then it is unlikely that he or she will suffer from a deficiency.

Below is a list of the key vitamins. Vitamins are either fat soluble or water soluble. Fat-soluble vitamins, vitamins A, D, E, and K, are stored in the body. Water-soluble vitamins, vitamins C and B group, are destroyed by water and are not stored in the body, so you need a regular daily intake.

Vitamin A: essential for healthy skin, eyes, and bone growth. It comes in two forms: retinol, found in animal products, and beta-carotene, which is converted into vitamin A in the body. It is also an antioxidant.
Sources: liver, eggs, dairy products, brightly colored vegetables.

Vitamin B1: required for the release of energy from carbohydrates.
Sources: dried yeast, whole wheat foods, oatmeal, whole grain cereals, pork, peanuts, most vegetables, and milk.

Vitamin B2: helps utilize energy from food and helps keep skin, nails, and hair healthy. Nearly half of our daily intake comes from milk.

Sources: milk, cheese, eggs, fish, liver, kidney, and yeast.

Vitamin B3: also helps release energy from food.
Sources: lean meat, liver, fish, eggs, whole wheat foods, and avocados.

Vitamin B6: involved with the metabolism of energy from protein.
Sources: brewer's yeast, wheat germ, bran, beef, liver, kidney, heart, eggs, milk, and cabbage.

Vitamin B12: helps form red blood cells and nerves.
Sources: beef, pork, liver, kidney, eggs, cheese, and milk.

Folic acid: helps form red blood cells.
Sources: leafy green vegetables, liver, and beans.

Vitamin C: helps prevent infections, and is an antioxidant.
Sources: kiwi fruit, citrus fruit, berries, green and leafy vegetables, and parsley.

Vitamin D: helps promote strong teeth and bones.
Sources: butter, margarine, butter replacement spreads, and oily fish.

Vitamin E: helps build cells and increases the body's immune response. *Sources*: seeds and seed oils.

Vitamin K: promotes normal clotting of the blood.
Sources: leafy green vegetables.

Minerals

Like vitamins, minerals are also an essential part of your child's healthy diet. Here is a list of the key minerals your child needs.

Calcium: vital for strong bones and teeth; helps your child's nervous system and heart to function.
Sources: all milk products and cheeses, salmon, sardines, soybeans, dried beans, and green vegetables.

Iodine: an essential mineral of the thyroid gland that helps maintain metabolic rate.
Sources: all seafood, seaweed and kelp, and milk.

Iron: part of the red blood cells that help carry oxygen around the body. A lack of iron causes tiredness, pale skin color, and poor, weak, and thin nails. Foods rich in vitamin C improve iron absorption.
Sources: red meat, heart, liver, oysters, egg yolks, beans, and nuts.

Magnesium: part of all cells, but very useful alongside calcium and vitamin D to build up teeth and bones.
Sources: all fruit and vegetables; also in meat, fish, eggs, cheese, and milk.

Phosphorus: most is found in the skeleton of the body and the balance can be upset by drinking too many sodas (fizzy drinks).
Sources: meat, poultry, fish, whole grains, nuts, seeds, and eggs.

Potassium: essential part of cells and important in nerve function.
Sources: found in all fruit and vegetables, especially in tomatoes, bananas, oranges, strawberries, and potatoes.

Selenium: involved with the heart muscles, infertility, and aging. It is also an antioxidant.
Sources: Brazil nuts, tuna, wheat germ, bran, broccoli, onions, and tomatoes.

Zinc: accelerates wound healing, and is involved in cell growth.
Sources: found in most meats, poultry, fish, peas, beans, and lentils.

Equipment & presentation

You don't need lots of special equipment to prepare healthy and delicious meals for your child, but certain items will help you to save time. You'll find these suggestions helpful if you are a busy parent with lots of demands on your time.

Essential equipment

Check what you have against the items shown here: these items will help you cook and present dishes more quickly or attractively for your child. You may find that you have most of them. If not, add them as your budget allows.

Steamer: steaming is a quick and healthy way to cook vegetables because it preserves nutrients that would be lost through other methods of cooking. A multi-layered steamer is excellent for cooking several foods at the same time.

Blender: if there is one gadget you should have in your kitchen, this is it. A blender will make short work of puréeing fruit and vegetables for babies, and sauces for older children. The alternative is pushing food through a strainer, which doesn't produce such a smooth purée.

Food processor: this isn't essential, but makes short work of chopping and puréeing large quantities of food quickly.

Cookie cutters: a selection of cutters in fancy shapes, such as circles and trees, will prove handy for cutting out foods into attractive shapes for your child.

Knives: buy the best-quality knives you can afford, because they will last longer and will perform better for you.

Apple corer: this will make light work of removing cores from apples and pears.

Cherry pitter: this is ideal for removing stones (pits) from cherries and olives.

Pastry (piping) bag with fancy nozzles (tips): invaluable for decorating cakes, cookies, and other treats.

Ice-cube trays and freezer containers: these are ideal for freezing purées and other foods in small portions. Choose freezer containers that have snap-on lids and that are suitable for transferring straight to the microwave.

Presentation

There is nothing quite like creative presentation to tempt the palate of a young child or fussy eater. Here are a few tips to help you capture your child's imagination.

● Cut open sandwiches into attractive shapes: for example, cut a slice of bread into a dog shape, then top with a dog-shaped slice of cheese. Add small pieces of olives for the eyes and nose, and a small piece of red bell pepper for the mouth. You could even tie a chive around the neck to make a dog collar and leash.

● Make funny faces on pizzas and tarts: cut pieces of carrot, tomato, and cucumber to make the eyes, nose, and mouth. To make cat faces, use green olives for the eyes, an olive for the nose, mushrooms, sliced and cut into shape for the ears, and strips of carrot, bell pepper, or chives for the whiskers and mouth.

● Put alphabet pasta shapes into soups.

● Make homemade burgers and fish cakes into fancy shapes, such as stars.

● Pipe decorative shapes or, better still, your child's initials in frosting onto cakes, cookies, and other baked goods.

● Pasta bows work very well for children, and if your child needs encouragement to eat more vegetables, why not cook some in a tomato sauce, purée the mixture in a blender, and use it to top the pasta?

● You can purée vegetables into soups, too, so try different combinations.

The only limit to what you can create is your own imagination. And if your child is a reluctant eater, let him or her help you with the fun parts of the food decoration and watch those tasty morsels disappear!

Get your child's day off to a great start with these delicious yet wholesome recipes. From fruity granola & yogurt parfait to spinach omelet, there's a fabulous range of tastes and flavors to satisfy both hunger and nutritional needs.

* **Scrambled egg muffins**
* **Mixed berry smoothie**
* **Strawberry French toast**
* **Spinach omelet**
* **Oatmeal with apple & raisins**
* **Fruity granola & yogurt parfait**
* **Blueberry muffins**
* **Banana pancakes**

breakfasts

Scrambled egg muffins

SERVES 4

Preparation 10 mins

Cooking 15 mins

2 tbsp/1 oz/25 g butter

1 leek, finely sliced

6 eggs

1 tbsp water

4 English muffins

4 scallions (spring onions), sliced

1 tbsp snipped fresh chives (optional)

salt and pepper

4 tomatoes, chopped, for serving

Scrambled eggs are a great way to start the day and if you add some extra vegetables they are even more delicious.

1 Melt the butter in a nonstick saucepan, add the sliced leek, and cook gently for 5 minutes, or until soft. Beat the eggs with a little salt and pepper and add the water. Pour the eggs into the saucepan and stir over a low heat until scrambled.

2 Meanwhile, cut the muffins in half and toast lightly. Spoon the scrambled eggs over the muffins, top with the scallions (spring onions), and a sprinkle of chives, if using, and season to taste. Serve with the chopped tomatoes.

GUESS WHAT?

Eggs are a good source of protein and also contain some iron in the yolk.

Alternatives

Add chopped ham or smoked fish to the muffins, then top with the eggs.

Add some sliced red or yellow bell peppers to the leeks and cook until soft before adding the eggs.

Mixed berry smoothie

SERVES 1
Preparation 10 mins

1½ cups/7 oz/200 g mixed berries, such as blueberries, raspberries, and blackberries, plus extra to garnish

½ cup/4 fl oz/125 ml unsweetened orange juice

1 tbsp maple syrup or honey

4 tbsp plain (natural) yogurt

2 cups/16 fl oz/475 ml milk

3 ice cubes

fresh mint, for garnishing (optional)

Smoothies are the quickest and most delicious way to increase your fruit intake, so add as many fruits as you can.

1 Cut any large berries in half, then place in a blender with the orange juice and maple syrup. Pulse to chop, then add the yogurt and milk and blend until smooth. Place the ice cubes in a serving glass and pour over the smoothie. Garnish with a sprig of mint and a few whole small berries of your choice, if using, and serve immediately.

GUESS WHAT?

Blueberries are full of vitamin C to fend off colds.

Alternatives

Kiwi Smoothie

Peel and chop 2 ripe kiwi fruit and blend with ¾ cup/3½ oz/100 g raspberries. Add 4 tablespoons of plain (natural) yogurt and 2 cups/16 fl oz/ 475 ml milk and blend until smooth.

Mango & Banana Smoothie

Peel, seed (stone), and chop ½ ripe mango, then peel and chop 1 small banana, and blend with 1 tablespoon of lime juice, 4 tablespoons of plain (natural) yogurt, and 2 cups/16 fl oz/475 ml milk until smooth.

Strawberry French toast

SERVES 4

Preparation 10 mins

Cooking 10 mins

4 large eggs

2 tbsp whole milk

2 tbsp superfine (caster) sugar

1 tsp vanilla extract

12 strawberries, hulled and sliced

1 tbsp confectioners' (icing) sugar, plus extra for dusting (optional)

2 tbsp/1 oz/25 g butter

4 slices white bread or brioche

2 tbsp toasted slivered almonds

GUESS WHAT?

Strawberries have lots of antioxidants to protect your heart.

French toast makes a quick and tasty breakfast—serve with plenty of chopped fresh fruit.

1 Place the eggs, milk, superfine (caster) sugar, and vanilla extract in a shallow bowl and whisk together.

2 Place the strawberries and confectioners' (icing) sugar in a saucepan and heat until the juices run. Remove from the heat, stir, and set aside.

3 Melt the butter in a nonstick skillet (frying pan). Dip each slice of bread into the egg mixture on both sides. When the butter is hot, add the bread to the skillet and cook gently for 2–3 minutes, or until just brown. Turn over and cook for an additional 2 minutes.

4 Serve the toast hot with the strawberries and the almonds scattered over, and dust with confectioner's (icing) sugar, if desired.

Alternatives

To serve with apples or pears, core and thinly slice 1 ripe pear or apple. Pan-fry in butter until soft, then serve with the French toast and honey to drizzle over.

To make spiced French toast, add ½ teaspoon of ground pumpkin pie spice (mixed spice) to the egg/milk mixture and serve with sliced banana.

Spinach omelet

SERVES 1

Preparation 5 mins

Cooking 10 mins

2 tbsp/1 oz/25 g butter

2 cups/2¼ oz/60 g baby spinach leaves

1 scallion (spring onion), sliced

2 eggs, beaten

⅔ cup/3½ oz/100 g crumbled feta cheese

salt and pepper

fresh sage sprigs, to garnish

8 cherry tomatoes, grilled, for serving

Omelets are very quick to prepare and make a versatile and delicious breakfast—fill with cooked vegetables or cheese.

1 Melt 1 tablespoon/½ oz/15 g butter in a nonstick saucepan, add the spinach, and stir until wilted. Season with salt and pepper to taste, then lift from the pan, and drain well. Chop half the spinach and keep the rest warm.

2 Melt the remaining butter in a sauté pan, add the scallion (spring onion), and stir-fry for 2–3 minutes. Add the eggs, season, and cook gently until the eggs are set.

3 Fill the omelet with the chopped spinach and feta cheese, then fold in half. Remove from the pan and top with the remaining spinach. Garnish with sage sprigs and serve with the tomatoes on the side.

Alternatives

Sauté 1 chopped zucchini (courgette) in ½ tablespoon of olive oil to replace the spinach.

Fill the omelet with roasted vegetables and crumbled feta or goat cheese.

GUESS WHAT?

Feta cheese is a great source of calcium for healthy teeth and bones.

Oatmeal with apple & raisins

SERVES 4

Preparation 10 mins +
30 mins to soak

Cooking 10 mins

1 cup/3½ oz/100 g dried
apple rings, chopped

½ cup/3 oz/85 g raisins

1 cup/8 fl oz/225 ml
apple juice

1 cinnamon stick

3 cups/9 oz/250 g rolled
oats

5 cups/2 pints/1.2 liters
milk

2 tbsp honey

2 dessert apples, peeled,
cored, and chopped

ground cinnamon, for
dusting

plain (natural) yogurt, for
serving

GUESS WHAT?

Oat fiber helps
lower cholesterol.

Oatmeal is a warming and delicious breakfast on a cold morning—serve with plenty of chopped fruit.

1 Place the chopped dried apple rings and raisins in a bowl. Heat the apple juice in a saucepan and pour over the dried fruits. Add the cinnamon stick and soak for 30 minutes.

2 Place the oats and milk in a saucepan and heat until simmering. Cook gently for 5–6 minutes, or until thick. Strain the apple and raisins and discard the cinnamon stick.

3 Stir the dried fruits and half the honey into the oatmeal and divide among 4 bowls. Top with the fresh apple and drizzle with the remaining honey. Serve with yogurt and dust with cinnamon.

Alternative
In the summer, serve the oatmeal with a mixture of summer berries.

Fruity granola & yogurt parfait

SERVES 4

Preparation 15 mins

Cooking 20 mins

5¾ cups/1 lb 2 oz/
500 g rolled oats

1 cup/150 g/5½ oz whole
almonds, blanched and
chopped

⅔ cup/2¼ oz/60 g walnut
pieces

1 cup/3¼ oz/90 g dry
unsweetened
(desiccated) coconut

1 cup/8 fl oz/225 ml
honey or maple syrup

½ cup/3 oz/85 g dried
berries or fruits

1 peach, pitted (stoned)
and chopped

2 cups/16 fl oz/475 ml
plain (natural) or Greek-
style yogurt

¾ cup/3½ oz/100 g
raspberries

¾ cup/3½ oz/100 g
blackberries

This recipe will give you more granola than
you need—just keep it stored in an airtight
container.

1 Preheat the oven to 350°F/180°C/Gas Mark 4.
Place the oats, nuts, and coconut in a large
bowl and pour over the honey. Stir until
everything is well combined and then spoon onto a
nonstick baking sheet. Bake for 20 minutes, stirring
halfway through. Cool and then stir in the dried berries
or fruits.

2 Divide the chopped peach among 4 serving
glasses, spoon over a little granola, and top with
the yogurt. Spoon over more granola and top
with the fresh berries.

Alternatives

Instead of the berries, serve the granola with some apples
stewed with a little sugar and a few golden raisins (sultanas).

Serve the granola with warm milk and extra maple syrup for a
warming winter breakfast.

Blueberry muffins

SERVES 12

Preparation 5 mins
Cooking 20 mins

6 tbsp/3 oz/85 g
unsalted butter

1²/₃ cups/7½ oz/
210 g all-purpose (plain)
flour, sifted

½ tsp baking soda
(bicarbonate of soda)

2 tsp baking powder

½ tsp ground cinnamon

½ cup/4 oz/100 g
superfine (caster) sugar

1 cup/8 fl oz/225 ml
buttermilk

1 large egg

1½ cups/7 oz/200 g
fresh blueberries

salt

3 tbsp icing glaze, to
drizzle (optional)

If you weigh all the ingredients for these muffins the night before you want them, they will be ready to bake in no time.

1 Preheat the oven to 400°F/200°C/Gas Mark 6 and place muffin papers into a 12-hole muffin pan. Melt the butter in a small saucepan, then set aside to cool slightly.

2 Place the sifted flour, baking soda (bicarbonate of soda), baking powder, and cinnamon in a large bowl and stir to combine. Add the sugar and a pinch of salt and stir again.

3 Whisk the cooled melted butter, buttermilk, and egg together in another bowl, then pour this mixture into the dry ingredients and deftly mix, but don't overmix. Fold in the blueberries and spoon the batter into the muffin papers. Bake for 20 minutes. Leave to cool, then drizzle with icing glaze, if liked.

Alternatives

Add 1 cup/5½ oz/150 g chopped pecans and ½ teaspoon of ground pumpkin pie spice (mixed spice) to the dry ingredients.

Replace the blueberries with the finely grated zest of 1 orange, ½ teaspoon of ground cinnamon, and 1½ cups/7 oz/200 g fresh raspberries

Banana pancakes

SERVES 12

Preparation 15 mins

Cooking 10 mins

1 egg

1¼ cups/10 fl oz/300 ml buttermilk

½ tsp vanilla extract

2 tbsp/1 oz/25 g butter, melted

1 cup/5 oz/140 g all-purpose (plain) flour, sifted

1 tsp baking soda (bicarbonate of soda)

1 tbsp superfine (caster) sugar

1 small banana, peeled and thinly sliced

1 tbsp vegetable oil

shelled pistachios, for serving

honey or maple syrup, for drizzling

GUESS WHAT?

Bananas are rich in potassium.

Pancakes make a delicious breakfast—serve them hot with chopped fruit and honey.

1 Place the egg, buttermilk, and vanilla extract in a bowl and whisk together. Add the melted butter and stir to combine.

2 Place the sifted flour, baking soda (bicarbonate of soda), and sugar in another bowl and stir to combine. Add the wet ingredients and stir well.

3 Add half the banana and stir again to combine. Heat half the oil in a nonstick skillet (frying pan) and spoon 3–4 tablespoons of the batter into the pan—each pancake will measure 4 inches/10 cm so don't overcrowd the pan. Cook for 2 minutes on each side and then remove from the skillet and keep warm in the oven. Add the rest of the oil and repeat until you have 12 pancakes. Serve with the remaining banana and nuts, and drizzle with honey.

Alternatives

Add 1 cup/6 oz/175 g golden raisins (sultanas) and ½ teaspoon of ground nutmeg to the mixture before cooking.

Place a few dried apricots and a little water in a saucepan and heat until plump. Drain and mix with a little honey to serve with the pancakes, together with sour cream or crème fraîche and toasted slivered almonds.

Try these versatile recipes for a welcome change from traditional sandwiches. They're great for lunchboxes, picnics, and barbecues, too. Vary the ingredients by trying different vegetables or cheeses—let your imagination run wild.

lunches

* **Funny face sandwich**
* **School lunchbox**
* **Three-bean salad**
* **Quiche**
* **Chicken quesadillas**
* **Tomato frittata**
* **Mini quiches**
* **Tuna pasta salad**
* **Vegetable focaccia**

& snacks

Funny face sandwich

SERVES 4

Preparation 10 mins

4 slices ham

4 slices white or whole wheat bread

2 slices smoked cheese, cut in half

1 slice salami, cut into 4 wedges

4 slices cucumber, cut in half

4 radishes, cut in half

2 tbsp ketchup

1 carton mustard and cress

4 tbsp cream cheese

These sandwiches are great fun and packed with good things—use your own favorite ingredients to create the faces.

1 For each sandwich, place a slice of ham on each piece of bread and trim to fit. Place a smoked cheese half on top, then use a wedge of salami for the "nose", and the cucumber and radish halves for the "eyes."

2 To finish, add a line of ketchup for the "mouth" and the mustard and cress for the "hair." Pipe the cream cheese along the bottom.

Alternatives
Instead of the ham, snip a few fresh chives into the cream cheese and spread on the bread before adding the rest of the "face."

GUESS WHAT?

Cheese is a good source of protein for growing bodies, and calcium for strong teeth.

School lunchbox

SERVES 1

Preparation 10 mins

2 slices whole grain bread

2 tsp smooth peanut butter

1 tsp strawberry jelly

handful of baby carrots, peeled

1 small container of soft cheese

small bunch of seedless grapes

1 fruit fromage frais with fresh berries and pineapple chunks (optional)

Be creative with lunchboxes and have a good mixture of fruit and vegetables. Add a healthy drink, such as a small carton of unsweetened apple juice, as well.

1 Spread one slice of bread with the peanut butter and spread the other with the strawberry jelly. Sandwich together and cut in half.

2 Wrap the carrots in plastic wrap (clingfilm) and pack with the soft cheese.

3 Place the above in the lunch box along with the grapes and fromage frais.

This is a suggested menu but bear in mind the following when putting a lunchbox together:

• Always include raw vegetables with a healthy dip.
• Always include fresh fruit.
• Avoid sodas (fizzy drinks) and have unsweetened fruit juice or yogurt drinks.
• Avoid potato chips (crisps) or salty snacks and instead include plain popcorn, mini breadsticks, or rice cakes.
• Always use whole grain, whole wheat bread, or pita bread, and cut the sandwiches into fun shapes if you have time.
• Use ham, cheese, mashed egg, drained flaked tuna, or similar and avoid any filling which makes the bread soggy.
• Add a box of raisins, a few dried apricots, or an oat and fruit cookie.
• Make everything easy to eat and have a variety of different tastes and textures.

Three-bean salad

SERVES 4

Preparation 10 mins

Cooking 10 mins

1¼ cups/10½ oz/
300 g canned
chickpeas, rinsed
and drained

½ cup/5½ oz/150 g
canned kidney beans,
rinsed and drained

2 celery stalks, chopped

7 oz/200 g green
(French) beans, trimmed
and cut into 2-inch/
5-cm pieces

juice of ½ lemon

3 tbsp olive oil

8 cherry tomatoes

½ red onion, thinly sliced

salt and pepper

This salad is a substantial and tasty lunch dish and also good to serve at a barbecue or picnic.

1 Place the drained canned beans and celery in a bowl and mix together. Boil or steam the green beans for 5–6 minutes, or until tender, then drain and refresh under cold running water. Drain again.

2 Add the green beans to the canned beans. Whisk the lemon juice with the oil in a pitcher (jug) and season with salt and pepper to taste. Pour the mixture over the beans and mix thoroughly.

3 Spoon the beans into a serving bowl and add the tomatoes. Scatter over the onion slices and serve.

Alternatives

For a more substantial salad, add some drained flaked tuna together with some cooked sliced potatoes and a few black olives.

Use a good mix of beans—try cannellini beans, lima (butter) beans, or black-eyed peas.

Quiche

SERVES 4–6

Preparation 20 mins + 30 mins to chill

Cooking 1 hr 10 mins

1⅔ cups/7½ oz/210 g all purpose (plain) flour, plus extra for dusting

½ cup/4½ oz/125 g butter, chilled and cubed, plus 1 tsp butter

1 tbsp olive oil

1 red onion, chopped

1 red bell pepper, sliced

1 zucchini (courgette), chopped

2 cups/2¼ oz/60 g baby spinach leaves

2 tbsp frozen peas, thawed

6 eggs

1 cup/8 fl oz/225 ml sour cream or crème fraîche

salt and pepper

apple and orange slices, sprinkled with fresh tarragon sprigs, for serving (optional)

This is a good way of serving a variety of vegetables in one dish.

1   Sift the flour and a pinch of salt into a bowl. Add the ½ cup/4½ oz/125 g butter and rub it in until the mixture resembles bread crumbs. Add a little water to bring the dough together and knead briefly. Roll out the pastry on a floured surface and fit into a 10-inch/25-cm tart pan. Chill for 30 minutes.

2   Preheat the oven to 350°F/180°C/Gas Mark 4. Heat the oil in a nonstick skillet (frying pan), add the onion, pepper, and zucchini (courgette), and cook for 5–8 minutes until soft. Melt the remaining butter in a separate saucepan, add the spinach, and cook until wilted. Drain well and stir in the peas.

3   Place a sheet of parchment paper and dried beans in the pastry shell and bake for 10 minutes. Remove the paper and beans and cook for an additional 10 minutes, then remove from the oven. Reduce the temperature to 325°F/160°C/Gas Mark 3. Spread the vegetables evenly in the shell. Beat the eggs, sour cream, and seasoning together. Pour over the vegetables and cook for 30–35 minutes until set. Serve with apple and orange slices, if liked.

Alternatives

Use a mixture of vegetables you like—try carrots, tomatoes, leeks, or broccoli.

Add some grated cheese on top of the quiche before baking.

Chicken quesadillas

SERVES 4

Preparation 15 mins

Cooking 20 mins

3 tbsp olive oil

1 red onion, thinly sliced

1 green bell pepper, seeded and sliced

2 cooked chicken breasts, sliced

4 wheat tortillas

7 oz/200 g soft rind cheese, sliced

4 tomatoes, sliced

4 sprigs fresh flat-leaf parsley, leaves stripped from stalks

salt and pepper

salsa or chopped fruit, for serving

GUESS WHAT?

Tortillas are a good carbohydrate, providing the body with energy.

Vary the filling in these quesadillas—they are delicious with meat, fish, or cheese.

1 Heat 1 tablespoon of the oil in a nonstick skillet (frying pan), add the onion and pepper, and sauté gently for 5–8 minutes, or until soft and beginning to brown. Remove and drain on paper towels, then mix with the chicken. Season with salt and pepper.

2 Divide the cheese among 4 tortillas and top with the chicken mixture. Add a sliced tomato and scatter over the parsley leaves, then fold each in half and in half again.

3 Heat ½ tablespoon of oil in a skillet (frying pan) and add one of the filled tortillas. Pan-fry for 2 minutes on each side until golden, then remove and keep warm. Repeat with the rest of the oil and tortillas. Serve with salsa or chopped fruit.

Alternative
Instead of meat, fill with grilled vegetables and salad greens.

Tomato frittata

FRUIT & VEG
FIVE-A-DAY
2

SERVES 2

Preparation 10 mins

Cooking 15 mins

2 tbsp olive oil

1 onion, finely chopped

1 yellow bell pepper, seeded and thinly sliced

1 zucchini (courgette) finely sliced

12 cherry tomatoes

4 eggs, beaten

½ cup/3½ oz/100 g soft goat cheese

salt and pepper

1 tbsp chopped fresh parsley, for garnishing (optional)

Frittatas are very versatile. You can make them with just vegetables or add some smoked bacon or sausage, if liked.

1 Heat the oil in a nonstick, ovenproof skillet (frying pan), add the onion, pepper, and zucchini (courgette) and sauté for 5–8 minutes, or until soft and beginning to brown. Add the tomatoes.

2 Preheat the broiler (grill). Season the eggs and pour them over the vegetables. Continue to cook gently until the eggs are set on the bottom.

3 Break up the goat cheese and add to the skillet, then finish the frittata under the broiler until golden and bubbling and set.

4 Scatter over the parsley, if using, and cut into wedges to serve.

GUESS WHAT?

Onions provide potassium and heart-protective chemicals.

Alternatives

Pan-fry some pancetta or bacon with the onion and add ½ cup/2¼ oz/60 g thawed frozen peas to the frittata.

Use leeks instead of the onion and beat 2 tablespoons of heavy (double) cream into the eggs. Finish with finely grated Parmesan cheese.

Mini quiches

SERVES 12

Preparation 25 mins +
30 mins to chill

Cooking 30 mins

1 tsp olive oil

1 cup/5 oz/140 g all-
purpose (plain) flour, plus
extra for dusting

6 tbsp/3 oz/85 g butter,
chilled and cubed

3 eggs

½ cup/4 fl oz/125 ml
heavy (double) cream

1 cup/4 oz/115 g grated
cheddar cheese

4 scallions (spring onions),
finely chopped

½ red bell pepper, cubed

½ cup/2 oz/55 g black
olives, pitted (stoned)

salt and pepper

Children love mini portions of food, so
tempt them with these.

 Lightly oil a 3-inch/7.5-cm x 12-hole muffin
pan. Sift the flour and a pinch of salt into a
large bowl. Add the butter and rub it in until the
mixture resembles bread crumbs. Stir in a little water to
bring the dough together and knead briefly. Divide the
dough into 12 and roll each piece on a floured surface
into 4½-inch/12-cm diameter circles and fit into the
muffin pan. Fit a piece of parchment paper into each
and fill with dried beans. Chill for 30 minutes.

2 Preheat the oven to 400°F/200°C/Gas Mark 6.
Bake the pastry shells for 10 minutes, then
remove the paper and beans.

3 Beat the eggs, cream, and seasoning together,
then stir in the cheese and pour into the pastry
shells. Mix the scallions, pepper, and olives
together and sprinkle over the pastry shells. Bake for
10–15 minutes until just set. Cool in the pan and serve.

Alternatives

Add pieces of cooked, chopped bacon.

Fill the pastry shells with roasted vegetables and
crumbled feta cheese before pouring over the eggs.

**GUESS
WHAT?**

Peppers are a good
source of vitamin C.

Tuna pasta salad

SERVES 4

Preparation 10 mins

Cooking 12 mins + 10 minutes to cool

2 cups/7 oz/200 g pasta shapes

2 tbsp olive oil

8 oz/225 g canned tuna in olive oil, drained

1 tbsp capers, drained

2 tbsp chopped fresh herbs, such as parsley, plus sprigs for garnishing

salt and pepper

bread, for serving (optional)

Great for lunchboxes, picnics, and barbecues, pasta salads are quick to make—use a variety of pastas to add interest.

1 Bring a large saucepan of water to a boil. Add the pasta, return to a boil, and cook for 10–12 minutes, or until *al dente*. Drain and toss in the oil. Let it cool, then season with salt and pepper to taste.

2 Flake the tuna and mix in to the cooled pasta. Stir in the capers and herbs and check the seasoning. Cover and chill until needed. Serve with bread, if liked.

GUESS WHAT?

Pasta provides complex carbohydrates to maintain energy levels.

Alternatives

Add chopped peeled tomatoes, pitted black olives, and a spoonful of green pesto to the pasta.

Add 2 tablespoons of sour cream, crème fraîche, or mayonnaise and a squeeze of lemon juice to make a creamy dressing.

Vegetable focaccia

FRUIT & VEG 2 FIVE-A-DAY

SERVES 4

Preparation 15 mins

Cooking 15 mins

1 focaccia loaf

2 tbsp olive oil

1 onion, finely sliced

1 eggplant (aubergine), cubed

1 zucchini (courgette), cubed

1 red bell pepper, seeded and cubed

8 black olives, pitted and chopped

3 oz/100 g mozzarella cheese, grated

2 tbsp chopped fresh herbs, such as rosemary

GUESS WHAT?

Red peppers have plenty of beta carotene for fighting infection

This is a delicious snack—add lots of chopped vegetables and a mixture of different cheeses.

1 Preheat the oven to 350°F/180°C/Gas Mark 4. Wrap the focaccia in foil and warm the bread in the oven for 5–10 minutes.

2 Heat 1 tablespoon of oil in a nonstick skillet (frying pan), add the onion, eggplant (aubergine), zucchini (courgette), and pepper, and sauté for 5–8 minutes, or until soft and beginning to brown.

3 Remove the bread from the oven and place on a nonstick baking sheet. Preheat the broiler (grill). Brush the focaccia with the remaining oil, then spoon over the cooked vegetables. Scatter over the olives, cheese, and herbs.

4 Broil (grill) for 2–3 minutes to just melt the cheese, then cut into squares and serve.

Alternatives

Add cooked sliced sausage such as chorizo, or ham or turkey slices before broiling (grilling).

Give your children their favorite foods, only this time they're healthy. From burgers to pizza, to chicken kebabs and tacos, there's a scrumptious range of familiar foods that don't fall short on nutrition. Many are also quick to prepare, which is very important when you've a hungry child to feed!

dinners

- **Meatball spaghetti**
- **Vegetable lasagne**
- **Tacos**
- **Bacon salad wraps**
- **Halibut with vegetables**
- **Healthy burgers**
- **Green bean pasta**
- **Vegetable pizza**
- **Chicken kebabs**
- **Cous cous with roasted vegetables**

& suppers

Meatball spaghetti

SERVES 4

Preparation 20 mins

Cooking 40 mins

2 tbsp olive oil

1 onion, chopped

1 garlic clove, crushed

1¼ cups/9¾ oz/ 275 g ground (minced) beef

2 tbsp fresh whole wheat bread crumbs

1 egg yolk

2 tbsp tomato paste

14 oz/400 g canned chopped tomatoes

½ cup/4 fl oz/125 ml vegetable stock

7 oz/200 g dried spaghetti

salt and pepper

fresh flat-leaf parsley sprigs, for garnishing

bread, for serving

This simple yet delicious dish is a good way to get your child to eat some red meat, which contains iron.

1 Heat 1 tablespoon of oil in a skillet (frying pan), add the onion and garlic, and cook for 5–8 minutes until soft. In a bowl, mix with the beef, bread crumbs, egg yolk, 1 tablespoon of tomato paste, and seasoning. Form the mixture into 1¼-inch/3-cm balls. Heat the remaining oil, add the meatballs, and pan-fry for 10–15 minutes until golden brown all over.

2 Mix the tomatoes, stock, and remaining tomato paste together. Season, then bring to a simmer and cook for 5 minutes until the sauce begins to thicken. Add the meatballs and continue to simmer.

3 Meanwhile, bring a saucepan of water to a boil, add the spaghetti, and cook for 10–12 minutes, or until *al dente*. Divide the pasta among 4 bowls, top with the meatballs and sauce, garnish with parsley, and serve with bread.

Alternatives

Omit the spaghetti and serve the meatballs and sauce with lots of steamed vegetables, such as broccoli, green beans, or stir-fried spring greens.

Omit the meatballs and add lots of vegetables to make a meat-free sauce for the pasta—add peppers, leeks, spinach, and serve with Parmesan cheese.

Vegetable lasagne

SERVES 4

Preparation 25 mins

Cooking 1 hr

2 tbsp olive oil

1 red onion, chopped

1 eggplant (aubergine), cubed

2 red bell peppers, seeded and chopped

2 zucchini (courgettes), sliced

2 cups/2¼ oz/60 g spinach leaves

14 oz/400 g canned chopped tomatoes

¾ cup/6 fl oz/175 ml vegetable stock

8 sheets fresh lasagne

1 cup/8 oz/225 g ricotta cheese

3 tbsp Parmesan cheese, finely grated

salt and pepper

You don't need meat for a great lasagne—this is a meat-free and delicious version.

1 Preheat the oven to 400°F/200°C/Gas Mark 6. Pour 1 tablespoon of oil into a large baking sheet and place in the oven to heat. Add the onion, eggplant (aubergine), peppers, and zucchini (courgettes) and toss in the hot oil. Roast for 35 minutes, or until caramelized and brown.

2 Heat the remaining oil in a skillet (frying pan), add the spinach, and cook until wilted. Drain well and squeeze out all the moisture. Place the tomatoes and stock in a saucepan and heat until thick, then season well with salt and pepper.

3 Spoon half the roasted vegetables and half the spinach into a baking dish, cover with 4 sheets of lasagne, and spread with half the ricotta cheese followed by half the tomato sauce. Add another layer of the remaining vegetables and spinach, then pasta sheets. Finally, spoon over the rest of the tomato sauce and ricotta. Scatter over the Parmesan cheese and bake for 20–25 minutes, or until brown and bubbling.

Alternatives
Use roasted root vegetables such as parsnips, carrots, and sweet potatoes rather then the peppers and zucchini (courgettes).

Add some soft goat cheese to the topping before baking.

Tacos

SERVES 4

Preparation 15 mins

Cooking 1 hr

2 tbsp olive oil

1 onion, finely chopped

1 red bell pepper, seeded and chopped

1¼ cups/9¾ oz/275 g ground (minced) beef

1 tbsp tomato paste

8 oz/225 g canned chopped tomatoes

1¼ cups/10½ oz/ 300 g canned kidney beans, drained

½ cup/5½ oz/150 g canned corn kernels, drained

8 taco shells

salt and pepper

salad greens (leaves)

2 tomatoes, chopped

4 tsp sour cream

1 cup/4 oz/115 g cheddar cheese, grated

These tasty tacos are extremely versatile—
try any number of flavor combinations.

1 Heat the oil in a nonstick skillet (frying pan), add the onion and pepper, and cook for 10 minutes, or until soft. Add the beef to the skillet and stir to break it up. Cook until browned and then add the tomato paste and chopped tomatoes and simmer for 30 minutes.

2 Preheat the oven to 375°F/190°C/Gas Mark 5. Add the kidney beans, corn, and seasoning. Stir and simmer for an additional 10 minutes.

3 Place the taco shells on a baking sheet and heat for 2–3 minutes until hot. Spoon the meat into the taco shells and top with salad greens (leaves), chopped tomato, a spoonful of sour cream, and a sprinkling of grated cheddar.

Alternative

Serve the tacos with a fresh tomato salsa. Simply, peel, seed, and chop 4 tomatoes and mix with ½ finely chopped cucumber, ½ finely chopped red bell pepper, and 1 tablespoon of olive oil.

Serve the tacos with guacamole. Just peel, pit (stone), and mash 2 ripe avocados with 1 tablespoon of lime juice and 3 tablespoons of sour cream or crème fraîche.

Bacon salad wraps

SERVES 4

Preparation 10 mins

Cooking 5–8 mins

4 wheat or corn tortillas

8 lean bacon slices (rashers)

2 scallions (spring onions), finely chopped

4 tbsp mayonnaise

salad greens (leaves)

2 tomatoes, sliced

salt and pepper

These wraps are perfect for a lunchbox or picnic. Simply cut in half and wrap in foil.

1 Preheat the oven to 325°F/160°C/Gas Mark 3. Wrap the tortillas in foil and heat in the oven for 5–8 minutes until warmed through.

2 Meanwhile, broil (grill) the bacon and drain on paper towels. Place the scallions (spring onions) in a bowl and add the mayonnaise. Season with salt and pepper and mix together.

3 Place salad greens (leaves) onto each tortilla and top with 2 bacon slices (rashers), the tomatoes, and the mayonnaise. Carefully roll up, cut into 3 pieces, and serve.

GUESS WHAT?

Bacon is a good source of thiamine.

Alternatives

Omit the tomato and add a few chopped walnuts, celery, and apple instead.

Add other chopped vegetables, such as raw carrot and celery, chicory, or mushrooms.

Halibut with vegetables

SERVES 4

Preparation 15 mins

Cooking 20 mins

1 tbsp/½ oz/15 g butter, for greasing

4 x 6 oz/175 g halibut steaks

2 tbsp olive oil

1 red bell pepper, seeded and cubed

1 yellow bell pepper, seeded and cubed

1 orange bell pepper, seeded and cubed

7 oz/200 g green (French) beans

salt and pepper

1 tbsp fresh parsley, finely chopped, for garnishing

All sorts of other fish can be oven baked—try this recipe with salmon or cod steaks.

1 Preheat the oven to 400°F/200°C/Gas Mark 6. Line a baking pan with parchment paper and grease with the butter. Place the halibut steaks in the pan, drizzle over 1 tablespoon of oil, and season. Bake for 10–15 minutes, or until cooked through.

2 Meanwhile, heat the remaining oil in a nonstick skillet (frying pan), add the peppers, and sauté for 5 minutes until soft. Season with salt and pepper to taste. Boil or steam the green (French) beans until tender.

3 Serve the halibut with the vegetables and scatter over the chopped parsley to garnish.

Alternative

Serve the fish with a simple sauce made with chopped herbs, such as chopped chervil and dill mixed with a little melted butter and lemon juice.

Serve the fish on a bed of broiled (grilled) halved tomatoes, brushed with a little olive oil, and a few sliced olives.

Healthy burgers

SERVES 4

Preparation 15 mins

Cooking 10 mins

2 lb/900 g sirloin (rump) steak or chuck steak

4 slices cheddar cheese

4 white, whole grain, or whole wheat rolls, halved

4 lettuce leaves

1 beefsteak tomato, sliced

pepper

condiments (relishes) of your choice

French fries (optional)

salad

Serve with sweet potato fries for a healthier alternative to French fries.

1 Cut the beef into chunks and remove any gristle, but leave on the fat. Tip the beef into a food processor and chop briefly to grind (mince). Season with pepper and divide into 4 portions. Form each portion into a burger about 3¼ inches/8 cm in diameter.

2 Preheat the broiler (grill) or barbecue. Broil (grill) the burgers for 4–6 minutes on each side—a couple of minutes longer if you prefer them well done. Allow the burgers to rest for a couple of minutes, then top each burger with a slice of cheese and broil (grill) briefly until the cheese is just melted.

3 Put a lettuce leaf on the bottom of each roll. Top with a slice of tomato, a slice of cheese, and a burger. Add condiments (relishes) of your choice if liked, and add the top of the roll. Serve with French fries and salad.

Alternatives

Omit the cheese and add extra salad and 1 tablespoon of cottage cheese.

Replace the cheddar cheese with feta cheese and add 1 tablespoon of hummus. Serve with chopped tomato or cucumber and olives.

GUESS WHAT?

Tomatoes are full of natural plant pigments for a healthy heart.

Green bean pasta

SERVES 4

Preparation 10 mins

Cooking 15 mins

2 cups/7 oz/200 g dried pasta, such as macaroni or penne

7 oz/200 g green (French) beans, cut into 2-inch/5-cm pieces

1 tbsp olive oil

1 garlic clove, crushed

2 potatoes, peeled, cubed, and boiled

½ cup/4 fl oz/125 ml plain (natural) yogurt

¼ cup/2½ oz/70 g green pesto sauce

¼ cup/1 oz/25 g finely grated Parmesan cheese

1 tbsp fresh basil leaves, shredded

salt and pepper

fresh flat-leaf parsley sprigs, for garnishing

This is a healthy way to serve pasta, with green beans and pesto.

1 Bring a large saucepan of water to a boil, add the pasta, and cook for 10–12 minutes, or until cooked. Boil or steam the beans for 4 minutes, then drain and keep warm.

2 Place the oil and garlic in a nonstick skillet (frying pan) and gently heat. Add the drained beans and boiled potatoes, and cook gently for 3–4 minutes. Season with salt and pepper to taste.

3 Drain the pasta and toss with the yogurt, pesto, and beans. Divide the pasta among 4 bowls, scatter the cheese and basil over, and garnish with parsley sprigs. Serve immediately.

Alternatives

Add some other vegetables, such as cooked peas or wilted spinach and 2 tablespoons of toasted pine nuts.

Use whole wheat pasta in the above recipe, spoon into a baking dish, top with 2 tablespoons of grated hard cheese, and bake for 10–15 minutes until the cheese is bubbling and brown.

Vegetable pizza

SERVES 4

Preparation 20 mins +
1 hr to rest

Cooking 25 mins

1¾ cups/9 oz/250 g
all-purpose (plain) flour,
plus extra for dusting

1 tsp active dry (easy-
blend dried) yeast

½ tsp salt

⅔ cup/5 fl oz/150 ml
warm water

3 tbsp olive oil, plus extra
for oiling

1 red bell pepper, seeded
and chopped

1 onion, sliced into rings

1 zucchini (courgette),
chopped

½ eggplant (aubergine),
chopped

1 mozzarella cheese,
thinly sliced

4 tomatoes, seeded and
sliced

4 black olives, pitted and
sliced

This is a great way of serving lots of
vegetables on a crispy pizza base.

1 Sift the flour into a large bowl and add the yeast
and salt. Stir well, add the warm water and 2
tablespoons of oil, and stir together to form a
dough, adding a little more water or flour as necessary.
Tip onto a floured board and knead for 5 minutes until
smooth. Place the dough in an oiled bowl, cover, and
leave in a warm place for 1 hour until doubled in size.

2 Preheat the oven to 475°F/240°C/Gas Mark 9.
Heat the remaining oil in a skillet (frying pan),
add the pepper, onion, and zucchini (courgette),
and cook for 5 minutes until soft. Knock back the dough
on a floured surface, then roll the dough into a circle
measuring about 10 inches/25 cm in diameter. Place
on a nonstick baking sheet.

3 Arrange the mozzarella over the pizza and add
the tomato slices. Spoon over the vegetables
and scatter over the sliced olives. Bake for
15–20 minutes, or until crisp and golden.

Alternatives

Add your own topping to the mozzarella, such as mushrooms, spinach,
broccoli, and extra cherry tomatoes.

Spread 2 tablespoons of red or green pesto sauce onto the pizza base
before adding the mozzarella and vegetables.

Chicken kebabs

SERVES 4

Preparation 15 mins + 30 mins marinating

Cooking 15 mins

4 chicken breasts, skinned and cubed

2 tbsp olive oil

2 lemons

1 tbsp fresh thyme leaves

2 zucchini (courgettes), sliced

16 cherry tomatoes

16 white (button) mushrooms, cut in half

1 yellow bell pepper, cut into squares

1 red bell pepper, cut into squares

salt and pepper

orange slices, to garnish (optional)

GUESS WHAT?

Vegetables do not contain cholesterol and are good for the heart.

Kebabs are great for a summer barbecue—you can also make them with just vegetables or fruit.

1 Place the cubed chicken in a bowl and add the oil, the juice of 1 lemon, and the thyme leaves. Season and mix until the chicken is well coated. Cover and marinate in the refrigerator for 30 minutes.

2 Preheat the broiler (grill) or barbecue. Lift the chicken out of the marinade and thread the chicken and vegetables onto 8 metal skewers. Make sure you press them well together on the skewer as they will loosen as they cook.

3 Broil (grill) the kebabs, turning 2 or 3 times, for 10–15 minutes, or until caramelized and cooked through.

4 Garnish with slices of orange, if liked, and serve each person 2 kebabs.

Alternatives

Vary the vegetables you use—olives, bell peppers, eggplants (aubergines), squash, or pumpkin all work well.

Make fruit kebabs with sliced banana, cubes of mango and pineapple, and seedless grapes.

Couscous with roasted vegetables

SERVES 4

Preparation 15 mins

Cooking 35 mins

1 yellow bell pepper, sliced

1 eggplant (aubergine), cubed

1 red onion, sliced

3 zucchini (courgettes), sliced

4 garlic cloves, whole

1 fresh rosemary sprig

3 tbsp olive oil

1 cups/9 oz/250 g couscous

9 fl oz/275 ml boiling water

salt and pepper

1 tbsp chopped fresh parsley, for garnishing

Roasting the vegetables makes them sweet and delicious—top with plenty of chopped fresh herbs.

1 Preheat the oven to 375°F/190°C/Gas Mark 5 and place a nonstick baking sheet into the oven. Toss the vegetables, garlic, and rosemary in 2 tablespoons of oil and season with salt and pepper. Spoon onto the hot baking sheet and roast for 30–35 minutes, or until golden and caramelized.

2 Meanwhile, toss the couscous with the remaining oil in a large bowl. Pour over the boiling water, cover, and set aside for 15–20 minutes until the water is fully absorbed. Fluff the grains with a fork.

3 Spoon the couscous onto a serving plate and top with the roasted vegetables. Scatter over the parsley and servem immediately.

Alternatives

Chop some hazelnuts or pistachios coarsely and fork through the couscous before serving.

Make a thick tomato sauce to serve with the couscous and add some chopped chile to spice it up.

Finish off a meal with one of these delicious desserts, which won't destroy your children's teeth. From fresh fruit salad to tangy berry cobbler or juicy fruit tarts, there's a great variety of tasty and wholesome treats guaranteed to satisfy sweet cravings.

desserts

* **Fruit salad**
* **Cranberry & walnut bread**
* **Orange slushie**
* **Berry cobbler**
* **Fruit tarts**
* **Rice pudding with fruit & nuts**
* **Raspberry yogurt**
* **Baked apples**
* **Fruity stuffed watermelon**

& treats

Fruit salad

SERVES 4

Preparation 20 mins

Cooking 5 mins + 10 minutes to cool

juice of 1 orange

3 passion fruit

1 tbsp maple syrup

2 tbsp water

½ tsp poppy seeds

2 kiwi fruit, peeled and cut into slices

1¾ cups/9 oz/250 g strawberries, hulled and halved

1 mango, peeled, seeded (stoned), and cubed

1 melon, peeled, seeded, and cubed

1½ cups/9 oz/250 g seedless grapes

½ medium pineapple, cored, peeled, and cubed

Mix up as many fruits as you like and serve the fruit salad with a spoonful or two of frozen yogurt.

1 Place the orange juice, the pulp of the passion fruit, the maple syrup, and the water in a small saucepan and bring to a simmering point. Remove from the heat and cool. Stir in the poppy seeds.

2 Place all the prepared fruit in a large bowl and pour over the syrup, mix well, cover, and chill until needed.

GUESS WHAT?

One kiwi fruit provides all the vitamin C you need for one day.

Alternatives

Make a berry salad by using a mixture of blackberries, blueberries, strawberries, and raspberries.

Make a pit (stone) fruit salad with sliced peaches, plums, nectarines, and apricots. Top with pomegranate seeds before serving.

Cranberry & walnut bread

MAKES 1 x 2-lb/900-g loaf

Preparation 20 mins + 2 hrs 20 mins to rise

Cooking 1 hr 10 mins

3¼ cups/1 lb/450 g white bread flour, plus extra for dusting

2 tsp ground pumpkin pie spice (mixed spice)

½ cup/4 oz/115 g butter, cubed

1 tsp active dry (easy-blend dried) yeast

½ cup/4 oz/115 g superfine (caster) sugar

finely grated zest of 1 orange

1 egg, beaten

⅔ cup/5 fl oz/150 ml milk

2 cups/9 oz/250 g cranberries

¼ cup/2 oz/60 g walnuts, chopped

vegetable oil, for oiling

salt

This is lovely warm from the oven or lightly toasted for breakfast.

1 Sift the flour, a pinch of salt, and the spice into a bowl. Add the butter and rub it in until it resembles bread crumbs. Stir in the yeast and sugar, then add the orange zest. Add the egg and mix.

2 Warm the milk until tepid, then add to the flour mixture. Knead on a floured board to form a soft dough. Add the cranberries and walnuts, and knead so they are well distributed through the dough. Place the dough in a floured bowl, cover, and leave in a warm place for 2 hours, or until doubled in size.

3 Preheat the oven to 350°F/180°C/Gas Mark 4 and oil a 2-lb/900-g loaf pan. Mold the dough into the shape of a loaf and fit into the pan, cover, and leave for 20 minutes. Bake for 1 hour 10 minutes until golden brown and risen. Remove from the pan and cool on a cooling rack.

Alternatives

Omit the cranberries and make the loaf with chopped dried fruit and ground pumpkin pie spice (mixed spice).

Replace the cranberries and walnuts with chopped pecans and dates.

Orange slushie

SERVES 2

Preparation 5 mins

1 cup/8 fl oz/225 ml
unsweetened orange juice

½ cup/4 fl oz/125 ml
unsweetened pineapple
juice

1 tbsp lemon juice

10–12 ice cubes

1 orange peeled

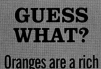

GUESS WHAT?

Oranges are a rich
source of potassium
and vitamin C.

These delicious orange treats can be made
with any fruit juice you like.

1 Chill 2 glasses until frosted. Pour all the
ingredients into a blender and process until
thick and slushy

2 Spoon the mixture into the glasses and serve.
Add slices of orange to garnish, if liked.

Alternative

Make the slushies with apple or grape juice instead of orange
and decorate with slices of kiwi fruit.

Top the slushies with chopped fruit or pitted (stoned) cherries
and add a splash of fruit syrup.

Berry cobbler

FRUIT & VEG 2 FIVE-A-DAY

SERVES 4–6

Preparation 25 mins

Cooking 25 mins

7 cups/2 lb 4 oz/1 kg berries, such as blackberries, blueberries, raspberries, loganberries

½ cup/3½ oz/100 g brown sugar, plus 2 tbsp

1 tbsp water

1½ cups/7½ oz/210 g self-rising flour, plus extra for dusting

½ tsp salt

6 tbsp/3 oz/85 g butter

¼ cup/2 oz/55 g superfine (caster) sugar

2 eggs

¼ cup/2 fl oz/60 ml milk

Greek-style yogurt, for serving

GUESS WHAT?

Raspberries contain fiber and lots of vitamin C.

This is a yummy, warming dessert with lots of berries. Serve warm or cold.

1 Preheat the oven to 400°F/200°C/Gas Mark 6. Place the berries in a bowl, add ½ cup/3½oz /100 g brown sugar and mix together. Add the water and place the mixture in an ovenproof pie dish.

2 Sift the flour and salt into a bowl. Add the butter and rub it in until the mixture resembles fine bread crumbs. Stir in the superfine (caster) sugar. Whisk 1 egg and the milk together. Pour into the flour mixture and mix until a lumpy dough forms.

3 Turn the dough onto a floured surface and knead briefly. Roll out to a thickness of ½ inch/1 cm, stamp out disks with a 2½-inch/6-cm cutter, and arrange over the berries. Beat the other egg, brush the disks with the egg, and sprinkle with the remaining sugar.

4 Bake for 15 minutes, then reduce the oven temperature to 375°F/190°C/Gas Mark 5 and bake for another 10 minutes. Serve with yogurt.

Alternatives

Use pitted (stoned) plums and blueberries and cook the fruits for 10 minutes in the dish before adding the cobbler topping.

Use 6 baking apples, peeled, cored, and sliced with ½ teaspoon of ground cinnamon and ½ cup/3½ oz/100 g superfine (caster) sugar and cook until soft before adding the cobbler topping.

Fruit tarts

MAKES 12

Preparation 30 mins

Cooking 15 mins

4 tbsp/2 oz/55 g butter, melted, plus extra for greasing

6 sheets Filo dough

¾ cup/3½ oz/100 g raspberries

¾ cup/3½ oz/100 g blackberries

¾ cup/6 fl oz/175 ml Greek-style yogurt

2 tsp confectioners' (icing) sugar

fresh mint sprigs, for decoration

These tarts are so pretty, you could serve them at a party decorated with a sprig of fresh mint—use any soft fruit you like.

1 Preheat the oven to 375°F/190°C/Gas Mark 5. Lightly grease 12 mini tart pans. Cut each sheet of Filo dough into 4 pieces and brush with butter. Place one sheet on top of the other and repeat. Press the dough sheets together and fit into the mini tart pans, make sure the dough fits snugly and trim.

2 Bake for 10–15 minutes, or until golden and crisp. Cool in the pans and then carefully lift each tart shell onto a serving plate.

3 When ready to serve, divide the fruit among the tart shells, top with a spoonful of yogurt, and sprinkle over a little confectioners' (icing) sugar. Decorate with mint sprigs and serve.

GUESS WHAT?

Blackberries are high in vitamin C and antioxidants.

Alternative
Use the Filo dough shells to serve fruit mousse and decorate with some mixed fresh berries.

Rice pudding
with fruit & nuts

SERVES 4

Preparation 15 mins + 15 mins to soak

Cooking 1 hr 30 mins

1 cup/6 oz/175 g golden raisins (sultanas)

1 tsp butter, for greasing

2½ cups/1 pint/600 ml milk

1 cinnamon stick

½ tsp ground nutmeg

¼ cup/2 oz/55 g short-grain rice

3 tbsp superfine (caster) sugar

¾ cup/3½ oz/100 g raspberries

1 cup/5½ oz/150 g pecans

1 tbsp toasted slivered almonds

GUESS WHAT?

Nuts are a good source of vitamin E.

A delicious creamy dessert, which could also be served with fruit pur‰ée or preserves.

1 Place the golden raisins (sultanas) in boiling water and soak for 15 minutes, then drain. Preheat the oven to 300°F/150°C/Gas Mark 2.

2 Grease a 1.3-quart/2½-pint/1.3 liter ovenproof dish. Place the milk, cinnamon, and nutmeg in a saucepan and heat until nearly boiling, then remove from the heat and cool.

3 Scatter the rice, sugar, and drained golden raisins (sultanas) into the dish. Strain the milk over the rice mixture and cover with foil. Bake for 1 hour.

4 Remove the foil and bake for an additional 25–30 minutes. Serve the rice with the fruit and nuts on top.

Alternatives

Serve the creamy rice with dried fruits, such as chopped apricots, dates, and figs. Scatter over pistachios before serving.

Serve the creamy rice with chopped apple or pear and a drizzle of honey.

Raspberry yogurt

SERVES 4

Preparation 10 mins

Cooking 5 mins + 14 hrs to chill

2½ cups/1 pint/600 ml whole milk

2 tbsp plain (natural) yogurt

½ tsp vanilla extract

2½ cups/10½ oz/ 300 g fresh raspberries

1 tbsp maple syrup

fresh mint sprigs, for decorating

This can be served at any time of the day— great for breakfast with some granola.

1 Set aside 2 tablespoons of the milk and heat the remaining milk to a temperature of 106°F/ 41°C. Mix the 2 tablespoons of milk and the yogurt together, then stir into the warm milk. Pour into a warmed, wide-necked thermos and leave for 8 hours.

2 Turn the yogurt into a bowl, stand in cold water, and whisk until cold. Chill for an additional 6 hours. Mix the yogurt with the vanilla extract and chill until required.

3 Set aside a few raspberries for decoration, then place the rest in a food processor with the maple syrup and blend to a purée.

4 Stir the purée into the yogurt and spoon into serving glasses. Decorate with the whole raspberries and mint sprigs.

Alternatives
Use strawberries or mango rather than raspberries or a combination of two fruits, such as banana and apricot or cherry and melon.

For frozen raspberry yogurt, make the recipe above, then pour the mixture into a freezerproof container with a lid and freeze overnight.

GUESS WHAT?
Yogurt is an excellent source of calcium.

Baked apples

SERVES 4

Preparation 10 mins

Cooking 45 mins

4 large baking apples, cored

4 tbsp golden raisins (sultanas)

2 dried pears or 4 dried apricots, chopped

4 tbsp chopped walnuts or pecans

juice and zest of 1 lemon

2 cinnamon sticks

4 tbsp maple syrup

2 tbsp brown sugar

4 tbsp/2 oz/55 g butter

4 tbsp water

plain (natural) yogurt, for serving (optional)

These apples can be stuffed with your own choice of fruits and nuts and served hot or cold.

1 Preheat the oven to 375°F/190°C/Gas Mark 5. Score the skin of the apples around the middle and place the apples in a nonstick baking pan.

2 Mix the golden raisins (sultanas), dried pears, and nuts with the lemon juice and zest and use to stuff the apples. Break the cinnamon sticks in half and place in the pan, then drizzle the maple syrup over. Sprinkle with the sugar and dot with the butter. Add the water to the pan.

3 Bake for 45 minutes. Let the apples cool slightly, then serve drizzled with the syrup from the pan and a spoonful of yogurt, if using.

GUESS WHAT?

Apples have lots of fiber to keep you healthy.

Alternatives

Stuff the apples with blackberries instead of the dried fruit and nuts.

Add some chopped marzipan to the dried fruits and use chopped almonds to replace the walnuts.

Fruity stuffed watermelon

SERVES 4

Preparation 20 mins

Cooking 10 mins

½ cup/3½ oz/100 g
superfine (caster) sugar

scant 1 cup/7 fl oz/
200 ml water

1 tbsp finely chopped
fresh mint leaves

1 medium watermelon

2 cups/10½ oz/300 g
black and green seedless
grapes

3 kiwi fruit, peeled and
cubed

2¾ cups/14 oz/400 g
strawberries, hulled &
halved

1½ cups/7 oz/200 g
blueberries

½ medium pineapple,
peeled, cored, and
chopped

This is great for parties as everyone can choose their favorite fruits.

1 Place the sugar, water, and mint leaves in a saucepan and simmer for 5–8 minutes, or until syrupy. Strain to remove the mint leaves and chill until required.

2 Cut the top third off the watermelon. Carefully remove the flesh in the melon with a large spoon, and remove the seeds. Use a melon baller or cut the flesh into chunks.

3 Place the watermelon flesh with all the other prepared fruit in a large bowl and pour over the chilled syrup. Pile the fruit into the watermelon shell and serve.

Alternatives
Use just dark fruits to stuff the melon, such as pitted (stoned) cherries, blueberries, and blackberries.

Index